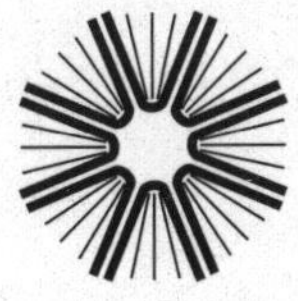

AF585489

Lisette

LISETTE

Catherine Rey

❧

GAZEBO BOOKS SUMMER HILL 2024

Gazebo Books
PO Box 375
Summer Hill
New South Wales 2130
Australia
gazebobooks.com.au

First published 2024

National Library of Australia
Cataloguing-in-Publication Entry
Rey, Catherine, author.
Lisette
First edition
ISBN: 978 0 6459209 9 4

Cover and interior design by Mountains Brown Press

Cover image: Rosemary Eagle, *A Quiet Place*, 2012, oil on cold wax, 28 x 28cm. Courtesy of the artist

Printed and bound in Australia by Ligare Book Printers

In memory of Lisette Nigot
15 December 1922 – 19 November 2002

In time, we often become one with those
we once failed to understand.

– Patti Smith

I

I awoke with a start. No light outside, no noise, but something wasn't right. Then I remembered my morning appointment at the pharmacy, to get my first shot of the coronavirus vaccine. Shaken by the thought that something could go wrong, I jumped out of bed and rummaged through my boxes to collect a few mementos: Lisette's last letter, her last postcard, her photo and the Parker fountain pen she had given me before I flew to Portugal, all those years ago. I sat down at my desk, picked up the pen, opened my notebook and pored over the photo.

Lisette, a short, thin woman, stands in the foreground, wearing a red jumper and white pants. Behind her runs a river; further back is a row of trees. She holds her white canvas hat at arm's length, as if waving farewell from the deck of a departing boat. Her round face is framed by the halo of her snow-white hair. Her lips mimic a smile, facetious and tragic.

Since Lisette's death, I've looked many times at this photo and each time, I've heard my old friend's voice asking: 'Have you forgotten me, kid? Don't you remember your promise?'

My promise? Should I call it my pledge? It was nearly twenty years ago, in August 2002. Lisette had asked me to take her for a walk in the nearby bush – more a strip of nature she and a platoon of environmentalists had rescued from the bite of developers. She grabbed a jumper before hopping in my car. Afflicted by Ménière's disease, she'd had to give up driving. I headed up the road, turned right, left, pulled up near a dirt road. Our stroll, even on flat ground, was unexpectedly curtailed just fifty meters down the track – Lisette had grown weary. Her heart, the 'old pump' as she called it, was a fragile one. We retreated to the car and headed back to her place. Once home, she boiled water in the kettle and filled up two cups. We sat at the dining table in the angle formed by the large bay windows overlooking the garden, a warm corner facing north, sunny all year long.

That day, as we were sipping our tea, she had looked at me intensely and said, 'You'll have to promise one thing before you leave Perth.'

'Of course,' I hastily answered, not knowing what to expect.

She was unusually solemn.

'I want to be in one of your texts. You'll write something about an old lady…'

She seemed deep in thought. After a silence, she added, 'An old lady who wants to put an end to her life.'

I nodded and said, 'I will.'

*

Since Lisette's death, I have postponed my commitment. In truth, I haven't written the promised text for the simple reason that I was unable to put pen to paper. I was forty-five at the time, a mature woman, yet I wasn't old enough to grasp what my friend was going through. Lisette's decision to terminate her life by way of voluntary euthanasia before she turned eighty was a choice I respected. When I flew back to Perth a few months later, I was told that she had kept to her plan by taking a lethal dose of barbiturates. An elderly lady who happened to be my friend had taken her life. What else could I add? People commit suicide every day, young ones, old ones. How could I write a book about it?

It took me twenty years however to realise that I couldn't fathom the rationale behind her decision. Upon reaching a season of life called autumn, or maybe the early days of winter, I look at the past through a different lens, and see that we seldom understand others. Their dilemmas, their pains, their silences, their secret wounds. We never fully understand even the people we love the most. The last conversation we should have had with them keeps haunting us for years because we should have listened, asked, protested, expressed our feelings, our love.

The awkward questions I used to ask my grandparents, with whom I lived from the time I was born to the time I left my country town to go to university, used to get just one answer.

'One day, you'll understand,' my grandmother would say.

My grandfather would nod.

This was followed by a prolonged silence while they both gazed sorrowfully into space. Thus ended the conversation. Silence was their answer; what they knew beyond any form of expression couldn't be conveyed with simple words.

With Lisette, it is not so different. Back then,

when she asked me to write about her decision as we were sitting at the dining table, she had divined that one day I would understand, and that on that day, I would be ready to honour my word.

Still, it took me nearly twenty years. Growing old is not what you expect it to be. One thinks it is about visible signs like grey hair, wrinkles, poor health, brittle bones or staying awake at night rewriting the past, but it is much more than that. Growing old brings the painful awareness that the people we finally understand are for the most part the ones who are dead. The last dialogue we never had with them, that lonely conversation we keep having with their shadowy ghosts as we grow old, brings us closer to the person they have been.

And imagination, however powerful, even for a writer, is of no value in this. Time alone is the teacher.

*

I met Lisette at a conference organised by the Alliance Française of Perth. Philippe Djian had been invited to give a talk at Edith Cowan University. He was the author of *Betty Blue,* an offbeat novel in the spirit of Jack Kerouac that had enthused a whole generation, including me.

As a member of the Alliance Française committee, Lisette always lent a hand. Standing near the door of a small auditorium, she welcomed people, addressing each of them with a polite word. There was a wooden box on the table in front of her into which she piled the tickets and the cash. I walked down the carpeted stairs and stood beside her. She raised her head to look at me, since she only came up as high as my shoulder. She was wearing a bottle-green dress, not a flattering one. Her lips shone with a discreet lipstick. I remember her smile. A quirky smile.

Marguerite, one of Lisette's lifetime friends and the Alliance Française president at the time, came over to greet me and introduce Lisette. Once

Marguerite had stepped away, ushering people to a seat, Lisette looked me in the eyes and declared she already knew who I was. I was Catherine. I was a writer. I laughed. Flashing her charming smile, she seemed like a good-humoured old lady, but as I reflect upon it today, I sense she was more of a lonely soul shyly asking another lonely soul, 'Want to be my friend?'

A few days later, Lisette invited me to her place, five minutes from the ocean. We soon realised we were *pays*, she from La Cotinière, a small town on the island of Oléron in the Atlantic Ocean, I from Saintes, on the mainland. In colloquial French, to be *pays* means to be natives of the same region and it creates a solid bond when you live far away from home, as it did for soldiers in the trenches.

Lisette's bungalow was sunny, open, unsophisticated, like a holiday house with plain, outdated furniture. Something about it had the feel of the French Atlantic coast. Mixed scents floated about – a blend of iodine, sea spray, sand, wet beach towels, sun lotion. When Lisette wasn't too tired and if the weather allowed it, she'd go for a dip in the nearby cove whose waters were 'rich in oligo-elements' as she explained very seriously. Crowning a small dresser of white Formica, an exuberant devil's ivy threw its lianas down the sides before racing along the skirting-boards of the kitchen and the dining room. Through the glass kitchen door, I could see garlands of nasturtiums in their tender dresses. They reminded me of those running between the paved path and the side wall at my uncle's house in Saintes. Each spring, they reappeared in healthy splashes of bright orange and tonic green. Each time I saw the fragile flowers bound to wither under the harsh summer sun of Western Australia, I grew nostalgic. The smells, the colours, the atmosphere. I loved everything there. Going to Lisette's was like being back home.

I quickly sought her friendship. And she quickly sought mine. In the eleven months during which I regularly dropped in at her place or got to meet her at the Alliance Française's congenial gathering, I grew very fond of her. She was one of the few people I could confide in with an open heart. Lisette could grasp anything. And she was a good listener. I remember talking at length – about my dysfunctional family which I'd gladly left on the other side of the world and about how much I had been struggling to adapt to a foreign country and a foreign language.

As I'm putting this text together, I realise that Lisette was born in 1922, the same year as my late mother. She died on November 19, the day that marked my grandmother's birth. The large veil of her beginning and her end was already enfolding me before I knew it.

*

Some days, we would chat. Even though she had lost her passion for reading, Lisette was more than happy to talk about literature. Other days, we would work on one of my manuscripts. Among other things, Lisette had toiled on an English translation of Paul Claudel's *The Satin Slipper*. It was no easy task to tackle Claudel's mystical poetry. But pirouetting between French and English had become a second nature to her. Back then, I had received the draft translation of my first novel *L'Ami intime.* When I mentioned that my command of literary English wasn't good enough to assess the work, Lisette immediately suggested, 'Bring it with you next time!'

A week later, as soon as we sat at the table, I pulled the manuscript out of my bag. She put on her reading glasses, started flicking through the loose pages and suggested a few edits. She mastered every nuance, able to juggle with a wide range of words. I was overjoyed. That's how we began to know and trust each other.

*

One morning – it might have been half-way into the last year we spent together – a letter from the Centre National du Livre, the French Centre for Literature, notified me that the grant I had applied for, and dreamt of, had become reality. It didn't take long before I felt like a prisoner plotting my escape, itching to leave Western Australia and especially Perth, really more of a dry, isolated country town than a capital, where I worked as a casual teacher at the local university. I made up my mind in no time. I wanted to go to Lisbon. That was it. The next destination would be Lisbon.

Within a few days, I had persuaded Thomas, who was to become my husband, that there was no other place than Lisbon, Fernando Pessoa's beloved Lisbon. Thomas didn't need much convincing. He was ready to leave Perth anytime. The house could be let go of easily, as we lived in a rental. We didn't fret about selling our treasures. Most of our belongings had been salvaged from the side of the road.

Overjoyed about flying to Portugal, I was also

dazzled, like a bird caught in a decoy. A friend had warned many years before that happiness makes us selfish. She was right. I was dazed by my sudden stroke of luck. Dazed and oblivious. Lisette never tried to delay my leaving though. Instead, she was happy for me, knowing how frustrating our lonely city was for a writer seeking inspiration. She herself had landed in Perth more by accident than by choice after coming across a job opportunity as a university teacher. A laid-back town on the Indian Ocean would be the best and maybe the last port of call, she thought, a place to unwind after a demanding career in the United States.

Lisette was glad for me; nevertheless, she knew we wouldn't see each other again. Such a realisation was buried too deeply in my consciousness. I couldn't take in the idea that *the big thing*, as she called it, was going to happen. I couldn't come to terms with the fact that Lisette wouldn't be around when I came back from Lisbon. All that I wished for was to carry on just like before, sit again at the dining table, pick up the pens, read the manuscript, flick through the massive dictionaries she had fetched from her study at the back of the house, look for the right word, hunt for another one, and make jokes in the meantime – an urge solely motivated by my need to keep her, to see her again when I came back to Perth, my need to carry on with our routine because part of me refused to believe that *the big thing* was going to happen.

But it did happen.

*

I had already heard about Lisette long before I met her. She was a well-known figure in our small French circle. Each time Marguerite talked about her old friend, she got overly excited, explaining, 'She's had quite an amazing life, you know!' as though Lisette's past was still shedding its wondrous light around.

Marguerite would subsequently explain, as she

had already done time and again, that as a bright Sorbonne student, Lisette had migrated to the States with an international fellowship, settling first in Chicago when she was hardly eighteen. She had earned pocket money by modelling for stockings, thanks to her well-shaped legs, ah! how thin and beautiful were Lisette's legs! and pursued a career at the Waldorf Astoria, ah! the iconic Waldorf, the luxury hotel in the heart of Manhattan, Marguerite laughed. It was the hotbed of the rich and famous of this world. Politicians, millionaires, movie stars. The Duke and the Duchess of Windsor for instance, well, they had an apartment there in the most glamorous part of the hotel. And Charles de Gaulle. And Salvador Dali. And Maria Callas. She's met so many famous people! She organised their press conferences, escorted their outings and complied, to the best of her abilities, with their whims. Soothing the anxiety of a diva who felt like rehearsing the last duet of *The Magic Flute* when everyone was asleep. Reassuring a moody movie star who craved a bottle of Bordeaux Mouton Rothschild 1935 after a sleepless night.

If Lisette happened to be around, Marguerite would inevitably ask, 'Why don't you write your memoirs, Lisette? You've met the Kennedys. You were almost a friend to some of them, like the Duke and the Duchess of Windsor. You took Marilyn Monroe to a department store. That's something! Why don't you write about it?'

Lisette answered, almost embarrassed since she didn't like to reminisce about her past, that she didn't have much to say about those people beside a few anecdotes. Yes, she'd befriended big wigs, including Charles de Gaulle. So what?

Marguerite sighed, burst out laughing and inevitably retorted, 'Ahhh, Lisette!'

*

Such was the legend. The post-war boom. A life of pleasure and freedom. Lisette's nightclubbing with

Bing Crosby. Charles de Gaulle enchanted by his young and witty chaperone he called 'the little rose of France'. Marilyn sitting at the Waldorf's bar, wearing headscarf and sunglasses, her cheekbones blotchy from too much drinking, poor Norma Jean waiting anxiously to go to the department store to buy a few pieces of lingerie with Lisette by her side. The subsequent commotion in the shop. The photographers rushing up the stairs. People screaming in exhilaration. Yes, such had been her life, but what I am about to write in the following pages isn't about Lisette's past.

*

I would like to try to capture something else, something invisible: a series of fleeting moments when Lisette and I were like two comets gliding side by side, close enough to cross one another's path while our courses had no chance to meet. I noticed something for the first time when she was granted the honorific title of Officer of the *Palmes Académiques* in a formal ceremony bringing together the French Consul, the entire Alliance Française committee and many impressive guests.

I vividly remember her mischievous demeanour during the evening. Whilst singing *La Marseillaise,* our national anthem, I had watched her clowning around, amused as she was by all this fuss. She had laughed without malice, for there was no malice in Lisette, no bitterness, no mockery. She simply couldn't help making fun of the world, because she didn't take the comedy of life seriously, the *Human Comedy* as disillusioned Balzac had called his body of work. She might have taken it seriously in the past, but not anymore.

Today, I clearly see how there was something incredibly impish and tragically lucid about her. Both at once. As she was fooling around, playing with the small silver wreath of palms attached to a ribbon she tried to stick in her hair, I could hear her inexpressible thoughts pressed against her sealed lips.

I could see how her eyes were filled with a mix of pity and disbelief as though she was leaving everyone, including me, on a distant shore. People adored her caustic sense of humour. I saw it for the first time as a polite mask. She had the gravity of those who are approaching death, a quiet detachment I've witnessed a few times in very sick people, in Hervé Guibert for instance when I briefly met him at the Villa Medici in Rome, shortly before his death. I was with a group of friends. He politely declined their offer to go downtown for a drink. I remember how calm he was, silhouetted against the bright blue sky, handsome and grave in his linen suit. There was a palpable zone of silence that surrounded him as though he had already crossed an invisible border and reached a land unthinkable for us, the living. Lisette shimmered in a similar void. Her body might have been there, yet something in her – her spirit, her soul or her true being – had already slipped into the afterlife.

*

My departure for Portugal was drawing near. We saw one another more often. I, feeling somehow like a dutiful daughter visiting her elderly mother. She, like a woman whose time was running out and who still had many chores to attend to before departing.

One afternoon, shortly after we had taken a walk, she asked me to make myself comfortable in the lounge room. Assenting to her unusual request, I slouched in one of the massive armchairs – the comfortable sort from the Seventies, wide, low and deep. She swiftly disappeared down the corridor and came back holding a cardboard box. She sat on the edge of the chair, turned sideways to face me, and opened the lid. She rummaged for a while through a stack of pictures, rebuffing the childhood ones where a well-groomed little girl stands near her sister Lulu. She finally picked a group photo, pointed at a young woman squeezed among tiered rows of students in front of an imposing building.

'Here I am!'

I drew closer to the edge of the chair to have a

look. The stately building blocking the view was her Catholic boarding school.

'Those nuns gave me a hard time, believe me! Tough luck! I've always been rebellious. One day I nearly set the place on fire,' she giggled.

The idea that she had almost burnt down the school delighted her. She paused for a while and kept fumbling through the box. I imagined her mind ticking over.

She paused again and picked up a set of discoloured Polaroids. Polaroids were one of the miracles of modern times: snaps that could be relished after a few minutes. Without a word, Lisette handed me the first one.

'This was on the terraced roof on my building. I had a duplex in central New York and a private terrace.'

The background showed a forest of chimneys. A blond girl lay on a sunlounge. She was wearing a strapless top and shorts. She flashed her thin bare legs, most certainly teasing the photographer by whispering the sort of words Brigitte Bardot would chirp two decades later in Jean-Luc Godard's *Le Mépris*.

'And my legs, you like my legs? And my feet, you like my feet?'

While I was looking at the picture in silence, Lisette produced more Polaroids. I scanned them one by one. The same girl reappeared.

She was twenty-three or so. Her curly mane fell loose over her shoulders. Her mouth was red, round and plump like a cherry. Her skin rosy, her waist thin, her expression cheeky. Owing to her small figure, she resembled a tiny Jessica Lange in King Kong's hand.

Transfixed, I couldn't take my eyes off the photos, riveted by the clothes, the buildings, the atmosphere of the time.

'Lenny took the photo,' she smiled.

'Lenny… You loved him?'

'Hm, I liked him. Handsome man.'

'Was he single or married?

'Oh, married... I preferred married men, 'cause they never stuck around for too long. No wedding ring. No in-laws,' she laughed.

'You never thought of having a family?'

'You kidding? I loved my job. I was making very good money. I adored my freedom and wasn't interested in having kids anyway. Listening every day to the same man who'd be asking: Darling, what's for dinner? Gee, that wasn't for me! At least with married men there's no surprises, and I had a great variety of them. And if they gave any sign of treating me like an object, they were out immediately!'

'And Lenny? Where did he fit?'

'Oh, Lenny was a gem. Easy going and good fun. A well-known chap in the film industry. Did I tell you what he did once?'

'Go on!'

'Instead of bringing me a gift, something I wouldn't like, he said, "Well, Sweetheart, you'll have to go to Tiffany's to choose whatever you fancy." Once there, I was walked to a table by a very smart shop assistant and shown a few pieces, within a range of prices of course, but you know, princely. I plucked one off. Not bad, hey?'

'And? What did you choose?'

'A large brooch shaped like a bow. Beautiful.'

'Wow, that must have cost him a fortune! Tiffany's…'

'I'm sure!' she giggled. 'But that's how life was in New York.'

I stopped flicking through the Polaroids. One picture had caught my eye. The same girl lay on a narrow day bed. The same stunning body of a young foal stretching her legs out in the air, half-turned to face the camera. The red dots of nail polish stood out like small jewels adorning the tiny hands and the adorable feet. This girl made me think of an actress – a very well-known French actress who became a Hollywood star… Martine Carol. Yes, she reminded me of Martine Carol with her round chin, her sensual mouth.

In the photo, child-like Lisette was putting on simpering airs, the way young people do.

'Who took the photo?'

'I guess it was Lenny… We were still together then. I look happy. We'd certainly just made love,' Lisette said briefly.

The Polaroid I was peering at made her smile. She gazed dreamily into space. She remembered where the photo was taken: her duplex apartment, shafts of sunlight pouring in, the narrow day bed where she lay. I could hear her meowing to Lenny, 'And my breasts, you like my breasts?'

She told me in the most natural way that she looked happy because she'd just made love. I could hear her words, yet they slid over me like droplets of rain slithering down the feathers of a duck. I held the Polaroid in silence. Lisette didn't add a word. If pressed, I'd say I was embarrassed. Faced with an unknown. I could hear her amused silence whispering, 'Yes, this girl is me. A young frisky me. You find it difficult to believe, don't you?'

She read me as easily as an open book.

We've just made love. Yes, I do remember being willingly impermeable to her words. The vision of this bouncing foal glowing with desire didn't match the person sitting next to me. Propped on the edge of the chair, her knees pointed toward me, was an old woman. Whom else would I see? I was forty-five, and I looked at the world, at other people, at life, with the eyes of a forty-five-year-old woman. What did I see? A wrinkled face, a thick waist, a spine slightly hunched over. Even if I professed back then to understand what I didn't understand – to sound smart, empathetic, woman-of-the-world – I couldn't get it. No, I couldn't get that there was no difference between the kinky Goldilocks and the woman sitting next to me.

Time exists only in other people's eyes. Time existed only in my eyes. The facetious girl hadn't given up. In the intimacy of this warm afternoon, Lisette was letting me know that she had, like any other woman, me included, once been young. She was letting me know that she had also made the most of life, rushed to the airport on Friday night, jumped on the Concorde to spend a romantic weekend in Paris to be back in New York on Monday morning. Because old people have been young, and they have done what all young people do. Didn't I know that? Was it a surprise? And today, as I am writing this text, I can hear Lisette's voice urging me not to conceal anything out of decency, prudishness or self-censure. Old people had a life, an adventurous, exciting, frantic existence before they grew old. Some might have run up and down the lanes of San Francisco to make it on time to a gallant rendezvous. Others enjoyed a quickie on the back seat of a station wagon, or in full view on the terrace of a penthouse. They might have had the craziest sex life one could imagine. Because, honestly, I haven't yet heard of anyone who doesn't enjoy a good shag in a parking lot, on the kitchen bench, in the shower or on a bed of soft ferns on a warm summer day.

*

A few weeks later, as we were standing before the full-length mirror down the corridor, the same awkward situation took place. Standing next to me, Lisette darted a complicit smile to her reflection before rearranging her hair by tugging at her meagre bun to fluff it up. Pretending that I hadn't noticed, I kept chatting away as if nothing had happened, unlike my grandmother who sneered when her younger sister readjusted her peroxide curls each time she walked past a mirror. The young sister was in her sixties back then.

How could I have forgotten my grandmother's alarmed cry for help when the threat of going to a nursing home was dropped?

'Help me, my darling!' she had screamed. 'I don't want to go there! There's nothing but oldies in there.'

She was ninety-one. We looked intensely at each other. There's nothing but oldies in there. Right. I got the message to make sure that she would never wind up in a nursing home. She never did.

How could I have forgotten my mother bellowing as she walked downstairs, dolled up in bright colours, 'Like my new top? Not bad for my age, hey? Seventy-three and a half! What do you think?'

How can I resent in them what I don't resent in myself? Like Lisette, like my grandmother, like my mother, I also see my younger self each time I catch a glimpse of my reflection. How can I be offended by my younger friends when they give me that swift look which always brings a fleeting smile to their lips, proud as they are to be in their bloom and unwillingly cruel, as young women can be, letting me know discreetly that I've tipped over the edge and now, sorry, I am the old one, the grey-haired one. And they aren't.

In the full-length mirror down the corridor, Lisette saw the doll-size pinup who didn't mind being wooed and loved making love. She sensed her young body still alive underneath her blouse and her white cotton pants, appropriate camouflage since when you are seventy-nine, you are expected to discreetly blend in.

In the looking-glass, today as yesterday, I see the long-haired teenage girl who wanted to be a writer, loved swimming and wind-surfing, lived at a fast pace, didn't mind being wooed and loved making love. Time exists only in other people's eyes.

*

I hold Lisette's talisman fountain-pen in my left hand. The pointy golden clip against which I rub the flesh of my thumb looks like the sharp Cupid's arrow that wounds the heart and makes it bleed with love.

My old friend is sitting next to me. She carefully piles the photos back into the box as we sit side by side in that warm never-ending afternoon.

'Tell me, Lisette, why do people talk about the different seasons of life as though we were closing a door before opening the next one? And one day all the doors are definitively closed. We are stuck in the last room, the last gloomy room of the old crocks.'

'That's the way things pan out, kid,' Lisette whispers.

'But where are the doors? There is nothing stopping us from walking backward and forward. Our mind does it ten times a day. Days glide over new days without us being aware of it because our true nature doesn't change. Tell me! Does it change? Do we change?'

'No, we don't. Being old is like having to wear a mask in a grotesque carnival. Whether we want it or not, we are forced to put on a deceitful guise.'

'The woman I was ten, twenty or thirty years ago is still here, well and truly alive. Have I changed? No! The past wounds keep pulling me back to the very same spot, the very same pain.'

'Deeps wounds never heal.'

'But my hopes haven't been trashed yet.'

'Lucky you! As for me, the time of hope and expectations is over. I've exhausted my supply. When I wake up each morning, there is nothing I wish I could do. Nothing! Thinking about tomorrow and the following day... See, I've had enough. But, hey, it's not sad, it's just the way things are.'

Lisette looks me in the eyes and murmurs, 'One more thing you've got to know, kid. The old woman glancing at her reflection in the mirror is the woman you'll become. Your body will fail you. My parchment skin will soon be yours and you'll disappear slowly. Eyes will pass over you without seeing you. You will shrink into the background until you become entirely invisible. No one will want to hear about your life. You'll end up being a non-entity, silent and resigned as if death was slowly drawing you closer. And you'll become one of those who aren't looked at as a woman, but as a relic, an antique, a granny, an old prune; the world has all sorts of names for the transparent thing you can collide with without noticing, a misshapen creature no one wants to become, not knowing that inexorably, inevitably, age does its nasty work like a rotten apple which ends up rotting all the glossy fruits freshly picked from the tree. That, you must know. No one can avoid the rot of time. Old age creeps in. Get ready.'

II

Facing a computer screen in a small internet café in central Lisbon, I noticed Marguerite's message as soon as it appeared. The first words were enough to make my blood run cold in my veins. Marguerite was letting me know that Lisette had passed away on the 19th of November. In accordance with Lisette's wish not to disclose the information before her body had been cremated, she couldn't write earlier. Friends, she also said, had gathered at Trigg Beach as Lisette's ashes were given back to the ocean she loved. The Indian Ocean. Stunned, unwilling to draw attention to myself, squeezed between customers sitting at the desks on each side of mine, I kept staring at the words while tears ran down my face. Lisette had done it. Lisette was gone.

It was a shock though it wasn't a surprise. Since Lisette's last letter, which I had received a couple of weeks before, I was prepared. Her detailed missive had forewarned me with such delicately chosen words that I have never been able to reread her farewell without crying.

Regarding the big thing I'm about to do, yes, it's still planned. And when you receive this letter, it's most likely (oh! I hope so much) that I will not be on this planet any longer, at least in my current state. … Then, kid, we'll not talk to each other – maybe, undoubtedly – anymore. This is what one should wish me.

Lisette's passing was bad news that I was expecting. Yet Marguerite's unadorned words ushered in a brutal reality I was yet to acknowledge. Lisette had died.

Holding hands without exchanging a word, Thomas and I walked back to our boarding house in a shoddy part of town. The city streets were brightened with Christmas wreaths and starry garlands. We walked up to our room, tucked under the roof. I sat on the bed, pushed away my manuscript and *The Brothers Karamazov*, which I had been reading. Our small garret window overlooked the front yard of the Pensão Viriato and further back, beyond the metal gates, appeared a section of the noisy Rua da Palma with its small convenience stores and tiny bar-restaurants. I watched the day unfold.

Lisette's thick letter lay still on the bedside table in its white envelope. The date stamp read '14 Nov 2002'. The night had begun to fall over Lisbon. The screeching of a tram up a hill could be heard in the distance. As it did every day around the same time, the pandemonium stirring our dosshouse from the ground floor to the roof top grew louder. Back from work, the day labourers were rushing up the stairs while the girls, dressed up for the night, ran down in a clatter of high heels, off to work as barmaids, pole dancers or escorts, slamming the front door of the *pensão* as they were leaving. Greasy cooking smells wafted up from the shared kitchen followed by the arguing between boarders as they wedged their saucepan onto the single stove. Although Lisette was dead, the motion of the pendulum hadn't stopped to weep and grieve her, but kept swinging mercilessly as it did yesterday and the day before.

Two months later, we packed up. It was a clear and cold February afternoon. As the taxi was driving us to the Santa Apolónia train station to catch our train to France, Thomas and I took in as much as we could of the tattered façades, the stone stairs winding up the hills, the churches we loved as well as the glistening waters of the Tagus, distraught to have to leave a city we loved.

Once back in Perth, I called in at Marguerite's. It was Pat who had found the body lying on the bed. On the wall was pinned a handwritten note that read: *After eighty years of a good life, I've had enough of it. I want to stop it before it gets bad.*

Lisette looked serene. A peaceful smile had brightened her face, Pat had said.

*

My old friend didn't mind mentioning the various ways of leaving she had thought about, methods carefully discussed with Dr Philip Nitschke and with the men and women who, like her, attended the workshops of Exit International to seek advice. Death by asphyxia required a plastic bag slipped over the head and carefully tied around the neck. There was the inhalation of carbon monoxide. Not easy to put into practice. Everyone agreed that barbiturates provided the most peaceful death. A good death. That's what *euthanasia* means in Greek: 'good death'.

Unfortunately, barbiturates and other powerful life-ending drugs were no longer available legally, driving people to buy whatever came along on the black market, or to fly overseas if they could afford it, to be given a lethal injection.

As for Lisette, she would take barbiturates. Sitting at the dining-table once our work was done and the table top was cleared, in a bright pool of light, we openly talked about the 200 capsules of Seconal she planned to ingest. She had stored several boxes that she'd procured when she lived in the United States. Their expiry dates being long exceeded, she had sent them to Paris to have them analysed by a trustworthy chemist friend. No nasty surprises. Barbiturates remain effective for years. That's how she would go. And that's what she wanted to talk about. Death by Seconal. She considered the step-by-step course of action, including any unplanned setback. One of these was the hiatal hernia sitting atop her stomach. Seeing that a haphazard mistake could make a botch of the whole enterprise, she kept revising the procedure while the cloud of a mishap hovered menacingly above.

Lisette talked calmly. I listened without trying to change the subject. With most people, she had stopped alluding to what was going to happen in the near future. Some harboured suspicions towards Dr Nitschke, whose name she hardly mentioned. She was also weary of those, the majority, who frowned upon her choice. She might have tried to convince them once. I imagine she would have made a point of broadening their views. Life wasn't black or white and many people felt unnoticed between the cracks. But persuading people wasn't worth the effort. Some people would never grasp what she intended to do.

Such an encounter with the grim reaper intrigued me. Lisette didn't shy away from it. Few people are utterly fearless in view of their prospective death.

In France, primary school children were taught the famous fable of La Fontaine: *La mort et le bûcheron*. An old woodcutter, tired of a life of hardship, calls on Death. After being summoned, Death comes along. As he faces Death's forbidding presence, the woodcutter isn't so eager to depart. *Better to suffer than to die, is man's old motto, near and far,* La Fontaine concludes. Most of us stick to this program.

Had any friend other than Lisette hinted at suicidal thoughts, I would have tried to talk them out of it. If the selfish half of me wished to keep her forever, because I loved her, the other half respected her decision wholeheartedly.

Indeed, Lisette's rationale elicited my respect. Putting an end to her life wasn't an old lady's whim nor a mad obsession. Her decision wasn't hasty or irresponsible. She mulled over it time and again. In retrospect, although I couldn't wholly comprehend her ways, I sensed in her solemn tone of voice, in her peaceful composure, in the realistic method she had planned, her courage, her determination, but moreover, her peaceful abandon.

She was walking to this rendezvous in the same meticulous manner we assume when we lock our house before going away for a long trip, making sure that the lights are switched off, the gas tap turned off, the back door bolted, the shutters secured and the front door barred.

My friend's composure was that of a traveller

ready to depart. I never asked her if she was fearful; the question was irrelevant. I never saw her breaking down. She never shed a tear. It wasn't haughty detachment, I can swear: Lisette was a congenial woman. Her logic didn't ring like that of a disciple of Epictetus who looked upon death with absolute impassiveness. No, she never assumed a stony-hearted attitude. She was still pondering over a few details: How long would it take to open the capsules? What day would she chose? What would be the best time? But she knew she would be gone before she turned eighty on the 15th of December 2002. She held it as a certitude. As for the 200 capsules of Seconal, they were at hand, waiting in a large round metal box.

*

I stand by your side in front of the mirror as you poke at your bun easily secured by a hairpin. I watch a smiling old lady, unable to read your smile and your silence. As I glance at you, you are glancing back at me. Is it a look of disappointment? Is it because you'd like to tell me something I'm still unable to grasp?

Today, shifting into the winter of my life, I can hear what you didn't say since the passing of time has taught me strange and painful lessons. Beside me, on a warm summer afternoon, you whisper, 'You've heard the expression "the weight of years", haven't you? But do you really know what it means? Time weighs. Ageing weighs. Living becomes an effort. My healthy life and my daily dip in the ocean didn't make miracles. I knew my old pump had had it. As they say, I've grown old. And Ménière's disease turned up one fine morning. The first time I fainted in the street was a shock. I lay there. For how long? I cannot remember… If it hadn't been for a man riding his bicycle on this back road, I would have stayed there. I cannot drive my car. I've got to ask you to take me for a walk in the bush. I've got to ask Pat to take me to the supermarket. I've lost my autonomy. I don't like the discrepancy there is between my mind which hasn't deteriorated and my body which is deteriorating. I will become more and more dependent on others. Perhaps my mind will go. And it if goes, what then? I'll lose control over my life. I've lived alone my whole life. I've never depended on anyone else but myself. I have always had a free-spirit attitude and now, doctors and experts are going to think on my behalf, act on my behalf and choose what is good for me. They'll decide to send me to some kind of institution. I don't want to be an object of pity or disgust rotting away on a bed. I don't want be a burden in a place where I can't move, where people make it their business to keep me alive against my will. They will stuff me with morphine and turn me around once in a while. That, I definitely refuse.

'I spent my childhood, say my formative years, around ordinary people, fishermen, fishmongers, day labourers. They surely weren't sophisticated, but all of them knew that dying peacefully is a great thing to achieve. They longed for a peaceful death. My grandmother prayed to Saint Joseph for a good death. But death wasn't a tragedy. Men risked their lives each time the boat sailed out of the cove. Funerals, processions, masses, celebrations: the church bells never got a chance to gather dust. Death didn't come as a surprise, because you knew you were going to die. But I don't want a scary, violent death, see. I would never be able to draw a gun to my head. I wouldn't be able to jump from the 10th floor of a building or do something violent because this is not the death I want. This is why I take the matter into my own hands. I was flung on this earth, but I'll leave it as I wish. And when I draw my last breath, I don't expect to be niggled by a grumpy nurse who'll ruin my good spirits. Because I want a good death, a peaceful death, the way people used to die in my small island.

'Still, I would have liked to have a friendly hand to hold mine. I'm not afraid, but I think it's sad to be alone at the time of death. You know that any form of assistance is sentenced? And if any friend stayed with me, that'd be considered a form of assistance and they inflict heavy penalties on anyone who helps or advises. And because I'm not terminally ill, I'm denied any help. The law compels me to die alone. Like a dog… Look at me! I am seventy-nine. I'm sound of mind. I am not depressed. I've studied and travelled and taught. I've never cheated anyone, still, the tactic is concocted to make me feel at fault. You want to die? Your call, but you'll do it alone. Yes, I have to sense to the very last minute the sting of my sin as they call it. Because I intend to take my life, and this is regarded as a sin against the sanctity of life. That's what they say… Anyhow, I'm not going to burn in hell. Yes, the time is ripe to die. I've sorted things out. Written my last will and testament. Organised my cremation. Paid the last bills. And I will not make a botch of it, believe me! I will not come back for a replay. No comeback. No regrets.'

*

Many have forgotten your name, sweet Lisette. Those who knew you briefly didn't notice the upheaval sparked by your death. The news took over Australia. In the leading newspapers, your picture beamed on the front page. The articles portrayed a seventy-nine-year-old woman in good health, but depressive, who had taken her own life after being manipulated by a man referred to as Doctor Death. We were explained that with some kind of psychological assistance, antidepressants, mood stabilisers, you would have been alright. If you had been admitted in the right institution, you would still be around to enjoy life without doubt. Reading such nonsense was appalling.

Your brilliant wit, your determination, the amount of time and reasoning you devoted to your rational suicide were disregarded and your truth was rebuffed because what happened on 19 November 2002 had to agree with what the government wanted to communicate at the time, what the Australian people had to hear and believe.

Lisette, I've been with you every day since I started writing this work. You certainly aren't any longer on this planet, as I've known you, but who knows if you haven't been hovering around? Who knows if your spirit hasn't been soaring above mine to pervade my dreams and slowly channel my thoughts closer to your truth? I wish to retrace your last days. I want to be with you in order to understand. My words will be shaped by what I would have done myself if I had to face what you faced, but I am trying to be true to your memory to help each reader make up their mind.

III

14 November 2002. Thursday.

8 am. Sitting on the kitchen chair, you stare at the calendar. No day could be more sickening than the anniversary date of your eightieth birthday. Four weeks from today. 15 December. Ugly date. How ugly. The numbers look like muddied soldiers falling one by one on the firing line, to the last one. You walk to your study to get a yellow highlighter. You'll give yourself four days to get ready, and you'll do *it* Sunday 17 or Monday 18. You draw large circles around the two chosen dates.

10 am. You flick through the phone book and search for the *S*s. You always had problems with the alphabet. S? Where is it? Here… Salvation Army. You dial their phone number, say you have a good deal of furniture and clothing to give away.

They put you on hold. Two minutes later, a man's voice tells you they will come Friday week. Late morning. The 22nd. You give your address and thank them. By Friday next week, you will be gone.

10.30 am. You call Pat. You don't want to ask anyone else but Pat, your soul mate.

'I'd like to tidy up the house. You mind giving me a hand?'

'Course I'll give you a hand!' Pat answers before you've finished asking. 'I'll buy lunch on the way.'

Fifteen minutes later, Pat stands at the door. She lives near the deli down the street. You look at each other for a while.

'Come on! Let's do it,' she says quietly.

Pat is a couple of years younger than you. You've known each other since you bought the bungalow, forty-four years ago. There was nothing here but a handful of shacks. A dirt road was the only way to the beach. Everyone knew everyone. It looked like a big commune. Pat lived in the house next to yours. She was slim, suntanned all year long, wore long colourful dresses. Every day, she'd wake up at dawn to go swimming. You loved the idea and you quickly became close friends.

Today, you will make a start on the bedroom. Any stranger walking in, including any police officer, must find a tidy place, to get a feeling of order. Because, that's how you are. A tidy, methodical and well-organised woman.

10.35 am. With determination, you start emptying the wardrobe. You put aside your two favourite tops, two pairs of comfortable pants and five underwear. You stuff five bin bags with your jackets, dresses, blouses and shoes. Pat grabs the blankets, pillows and bed linens. While she drags the lot through the front door, ready to be taken away by the Salvation Army, you glance at your car gathering dust under the carport.

12 pm. In the kitchen, you eat the sandwiches Pat has bought. Her eyes, incidentally, have met the calendar. As she stares at the two highlighted dates, she grows livid. You sip your glass of orange juice in silence, stand without a word and disappear down the corridor. Pat follows you into your study.

1pm. You've already given a good share of your library to the University of Western Australia. What's left is stacked in carboard boxes. You've got a good supply of cardboard boxes. For the last six months, each time Pat and you have been to the supermarket, you brought back a large one. You empty the drawers and shelves. You carelessly snatch your personal correspondence, driver's license, passport, all the mementos you were attached to, your *Palmes Académiques*, your notebooks and your degrees. They meant a lot to you, but don't mean anything to anyone else. You stop yourself from looking at any memorabilia, any letter, especially the photos. Throwing stuff away helps. It is a way to slowly dissolve your being, piece by piece. There is a difference between knowing the path and walking the path, you heard once. This is true. Walking the path is what you are doing right now. Pat has wheeled the two large plastic bins down the side of the house. Four bin bags crammed with your bills, bank statements and a lifetime of correspondence vanish inside.

5 pm. Pat is drenched in sweat. Your hair sticks to your nape. Worn out by a day's work, you are both edgy and pale. You sit for a while before walking Pat to the door.

'See you tomorrow, Pat!'

'I'll be here…'

'Hang on! The Salvos' truck is coming next week, on the 22nd. Late morning.'

'Hmm… next week,' she sighs while looking away. 'I'll be here.'

7 pm. The temperature has cooled down. You have a large glass of gin and tonic before going to bed.

15 November. Friday.

8 am. You've already started on the bathroom when Pat walks in.

'Let me put the sandwiches in the fridge, and I'll be with you!' she yells.

Now that the bathroom has been cleared, you start emptying the contents of the fridge. You leave two sandwiches, a bottle of milk and a bottle of orange juice. You hand over piles of plates, glasses, cutlery and saucepans to Pat who piles them into cardboard boxes. You've put aside on the dresser what you'll need: the kettle, a bowl, a water jug, five glasses, two teaspoons and your pocket knife.

12 pm. You lunch in the kitchen. Neither of you feels like talking. You exchange glances from time

to time. Pat tries her best to smile. Grief is written all over her face.

1 pm. 'Could you record a new message on the answering machine?' you ask Pat while handing her a piece of paper. 'Your voice, hey, better than mine…'

'Let's do it, Liz!'

'Here is what I'd like you to say.'

Pat nods, shakes her head, grabs the phone and records the new message: *I am sorry. Lisette has gone on a trip and will not be returning.*

'Thank you!'

Sitting at the dining table you look at the photo Pat took a few weeks before. It was a sunny day. You stand in the foreground. Behind runs the Swan River. Further back a row of trees. You are happy with the way you wave your canvas hat. Looks like you are saying: 'Time to go!'

'I'd like it to be printed on a double card,' you suggest. 'At the bottom my name and two dates,

15 December 1922 to…'

'What would you like to have printed on the other side?'

'When my niece Catherine called in last week, we put together a few words: *Lisette died at home in her sleep on… Her wish was that her death not be announced until after her cremation.* Signed by Catherine and her husband.'

'What about the opposite page?'

'Yes, what about the opposite page?'

'Something like *She leaves a huge contingent of friends in many parts of the world. We shall miss her.* Signed by Pat.'

You laugh quietly and thank her. You'll store her nice words in your thoughts. You hand her a list of friends to whom the card should be sent.

'Let me get a document!'

You walk to your bedroom to fetch a large white envelope bearing the address of the University of Western Australia. Inside is a typed document, carefully stapled. Once more, you flick through it.

It states that once a year, a scholarship of $8000 will be granted to outstanding students from your own funds.

'Could you make sure that I haven't forgotten anything. It's awful, I keep forgetting things…'

'Well, let's have a look,' Pat says while leafing meticulously through the pages.

'Here, Liz, you need to sign this page. Here.'

'Gosh! I'm losing it.'

While you sign, Pat looks at you. She knows you better than anyone else, guesses your thoughts, anticipates your desires, laughs at your jokes. She looks at your hand firmly holding the pen. Your signature. Your clear handwriting. She can feel the burning sensation of the tears coming to her eyes, bites her lips hard, looks away to the garden where the nasturtiums have withered. You hand back the document. She slips it into the envelope before sealing it. Glancing at her watch, she jumps to her feet, picks up the envelope and rushes to the door. If she wants to drop it at the post office before it closes, she'd better get going.

'See you tomorrow!' Pat says as she leaves.

'See you tomorrow, Pat!'

Once alone, you walk around the house. Empty shelves. Empty cupboards. Empty drawers. You nod. You did the right thing. You've kept a Spartan lifestyle since you moved here. It was judicious to do so.

16 November. Saturday.

8 am. Today is Saint Marguerite's Day, so says the calendar. You think of calling Marguerite. She has been a loyal friend over the years. But talking to anyone now isn't a good idea. You don't even want to go outside to water the garden in case you catch sight of a neighbour. You would have to wave. Would have to say hello. Thinking about it makes you sick.

10 am. The heat is unbearable. You have a shower, two sleeping pills and a large glass of gin and tonic to quell your anxiety, and go back to bed.

2 pm. Pat walks into the bedroom. You awaken out of sorts.

'You alright, Liz? You sure everything is alright?'

she asks with a quivering voice.

'Yeah! All right…'

You tumble out of bed, rummage through your hand bag, give her a box.

'Pat, you'll give that to my niece, please! I've put in all of my jewellery that's worth anything.'

You also fetch the keys of your car, walk Pat to the front door, slip them in her hand: 'It's yours now!'

As Pat is about to walk away, she stops, comes back. You hug one another for a long time. As you stare at her, she stares back at you. You sigh. She sighs and you both start crying in silence while gazing at each other without uttering a word.

17 November. Sunday.

6 am. You don't feel like doing *it* today. You never procrastinate. It's not like you. But you feel suddenly tired, overwhelmed, nauseated by the whole thing. Today, you'll write the note you intend to pin on the wall of your bedroom. You'll keep it short. A brief and clear message. You scrawl a few sentences and finally opt for these ones: *After eighty years of a good life, I've had enough of it. I want to stop it before it gets bad.*

10 am. You go through what you'll have to do again and make sure you haven't overlooked anything. You've got to be more mindful. Why do you forget? Why is that? Like the bill for your cremation. You fail to recall if you've paid it. And you cannot recall choosing an urn either. You

can see the woman you talked to: a middle-aged woman, her face, her hairdo, blonde, a short bob, but what else did she say? The urn? There was a catalogue on the table. Which one did you choose? In what sort of container will they put your ashes? Why did you let it slip? You are suddenly angry at the indomitable task waiting ahead you, tragic and meaningless and empty. You would like it to be over, done. You want to be gone. Forever.

12 pm. You think of calling Pat to ask her if you've paid the bill for the cremation. You pick up the handset, start dialling her number and suddenly stop. Does it matter? Pat will see to it. You know that. You put the phone down. Your heart is heavy.

2 pm. You walk slowly from the front door to the back door. From the back door to the front door. It's Sunday. You hear the neighbours getting ready to go to the beach. People laugh. Children laugh. Cars drive past. It's Sunday. The world is happy.

You don't know what to do with yourself. You feel like crying. You have a straight gin, two sleeping pills and decide to go back to bed.

18 November. Monday.

6.30 am. You open your eyes. This evening, you'll be lying here, in the very same place. This evening, you will be dead. The minute you woke up, you knew it. You walk into the kitchen, make a cup of chamomile tea, sit and glance at the calendar. Monday. 18 November. At what time? Far too hot and too busy during the day. Past midnight, no one will think of knocking at your door. No one will bother you on the phone. People will be watching television or asleep. And the temperature will have dropped. You brace yourself, having to endure through your last day, however long, with nothing to distract you from what is waiting ahead. Whatever thought crosses your mind, you cannot help going back to *it*, like iron filings drawn to a magnet. It will be a long day. More than eighteen hours to wait, and not much to do. Seventy-nine years have gone by in a blink, and now, your last day will go on forever.

9 am. It's getting hot. You could go back to the bedroom, or to your study. It's cooler at the back. But what if you pass out? Stepping away from the kitchen means taking risks. Small risks, of course. It hasn't happened lately. But what about having a fall in the study? For now, you decide to stay put on the kitchen chair.

10.30 am. You are getting impatient. You won't be able to stay still for much longer. The back office is the best place to wait. You'll be able to muster your strength there. You walk down the corridor, sink into the armchair and listen to the parrots squawking on the terrace outside. They cling to the metal screen, flattened like moths. They want their daily ration of seeds. There are no seeds left.

1 pm. You feel peckish. In a few hours, this body of yours will be gone, and it's still asking for food. Life is a nonsensical farce. You walk slowly back to the kitchen. Nothing much left. The two sandwiches in the fridge.

2 pm. You'll have to get dressed. Later. You chew the soggy bread and look at your bare feet, your grey toe nails, your protruding veins, your dry skin, your bony knees and look out to the garden. You haven't watered it for days. There is hardly anything left of the nasturtiums. Every year, the poor things get fried. Only the rugged natives survive the summer heat, with their dust-coloured leaves as stiff as cardboard.

3 pm. On the kitchen wall, the hands of the clock have halted. Your armpits are sticky. Drops of sweat run down your back. You wipe your face and neck with the tea towel.

3.30 pm. You must have a shower. Stuck to the chair, you cannot move. Your night gown is glued to your body. What about lying down on the cold floor? Just for a little while, time to rest. It's dreadfully hot. You wriggle to the front of the chair, bend over, stretch your arms, secure your right hand on the floor, let your body slowly slip onto the right hip, sit, and lie down before stretching your legs. The floor is cool. You remember lying thus when you were in Morocco once. The night was stifling. You couldn't sleep. You'd slipped off the bed to stretch on the tiles in a pool of coolness. You remember how you whole body unrolled easily, how your hip didn't hurt, how the tiles welcomed the whole of you, how you easily turned over on to your stomach looking for a fresher spot. How old where you? Twenty-five? Thirty-five?

4 pm. You've dozed off. You wake up to the screaming of children. The last school bus is thundering up the street. You gaze at the ceiling

for a while. It is stained and ugly. You give the clock a sly look. The hands slog around, unable to catch up with each other.

7 pm. Time to have a shower and get dressed. You try to get up to your feet, roll onto one side, push up on your forearms, try a second time, a third time, hold on to the rung of the chair, manage to stand up. You wash your hair with what's left of the soap. You want to be smartly dressed. You've chosen a white top and white cotton pants.

8 pm. You prepare a chamomile tea before displaying what you need on the table. The water jug, two teaspoons, five glasses. And the large metal container which holds the boxes of barbiturates. You put the 200 capsules in front of you in a heap, look at them as though you were dreaming. 200 capsules of Seconal is a lot. Well over the lethal dose. You are steadying yourself, ready to break their shells. You hold the first one firmly. It's

harder than you imagined. You might need to use something sharp and put a bowl underneath.

Sweat pours down your neck. You try again to open the capsule. Your hands are clammy. The capsule slips away. The old shell has hardened. You definitively need your pocket knife. You slice each capsule through the middle. It takes ages. You keep emptying more capsules into the bowl. It slowly starts to fill up. Now, you scoop the whitish powder with a spoon and fill a first glass. To this white dust, you add some water from the jug. You stir till it slowly turns into a thick odourless mixture. You keep slicing more capsules with the forbearance of a foot soldier, then fill a second glass. You'll need a third glass. Once done, you prepare a glass of vodka flavoured with orange juice. You'll drink it after. You display the four glasses on a tray. A last glance at the clock.

11 pm. Holding the tray firmly in both hands, you walk slowly to the bedroom, a few steps away. You pause for a while before placing the tray on the bedside table. You don't want to turn the fan on. No noise. First, you pin to the wall the note you've kept in your bedside table. You sit on the edge of the bed. Your right hand is trembling. Suddenly, both hands begin to shake uncontrollably. You close your eyes, breathe deeply, slowly. The sight of the mixture in the three glasses chills you. You stare at the mixture. The whitish concoction is also staring back at you. Remain as calm as possible, you tell yourself. No panic. The ocean roars afar. You listen to the crashing of the waves, the good and pleasant beat of the ocean, the rhythm you were born with, the rhythm you grew up with. The first rhythm you heard in your mother's womb. You don't feel the heat now. Curiously, the temperature seems to have dropped. The reality is brutal. For you, suicide means being in your empty bedroom alone, swallowing the lethal mixture alone, dying

in the quiet of the night alone. Right now, you hurt. Your lassitude weighs as if pushing you right down into the ground.

1 am. Still sitting on the edge of the bed you think that now, you must be valiant. You don't want to botch it. You don't want to add to the long list of failed suicide attempts. You must not fail. *Once I've swallowed the stuff, no turning back. I'll fall asleep for good in two minutes*, you wrote in the last letter you sent me. You hold the first glass with both hands and sips its contents. It sticks to the lips, the tongue, the teeth, the palate. You fear you will not be able to retain the mixture. You still run the risk of passing out. You moan while sipping the second one. As soon as you've absorbed the third, you let your body droop across the pillow. You have enough time to stretch out your legs, no time to flick off your shoes. The mixture has left a nasty taste in your mouth. Your breathing is heavy. You'd wish to wet your lips. You'd love a sip of vodka,

to kill the nauseating taste. You extend your right arm. The glass is too far. Its surface feels oily. You play with it for a while until it moves sideways, tips over the edge of the tray. Its contents splash on the carpet. You hear the sound. The strong whiff rises and vanishes. You lie still now and breathe calmly. You know how important it is to be quiet before slipping away peacefully. Like a drop getting back to the ocean. You've always known so. After all, it all went well, you think. It all went as you wished. Tears well up in your eyes. Yes, it all went very well. Like a drop returning to the ocean. On your deathbed, you smile. You have faced your destiny. Proven your words by your actions. You did so. You are soaring high to your last abode. You are leaving your body. Our planet. Us. You have swallowed death and you smile. Was it pleasurable? Yes, it was. Now you are reaching the place where you wanted to go.

IV

On the 1st of November 2021, I watched with an underlying anxiety the ninety-minute documentary *Mademoiselle and the Doctor*, shot by the Australian filmmaker Janine Hosking. Mademoiselle is Lisette. The doctor, Philip Nitschke.

Watching the film had to be done. The first three chapters of my book were already written. I felt somehow that my task hadn't been completed. How could I be certain that I hadn't missed any crucial elements? While reading again the last letter I received from Lisette, I realised that she had given me the information I would need to write about her well-thought-out plan of dying when, how and where she had decided to. Like the *Petit Poucet* of the tale who leaves a trail of white pebbles behind him to find his way back home, the path was there for me to follow when the time came. I could always go back to her letter to be reminded of the number of capsules she intended to ingest, her fear of the moment when she would have to swallow their content, her mention of the hernia that could interfere with her plan, her encounter with Philip Nitschke, the strong friendship that ensued and the documentary shot in October 2002 by Janine Hosking and her crew. The documentary was intentionally mentionned. I needed to watch it. What Lisette had in mind when she put together her last missive to me – four long handwritten pages that would have taken her time and effort – had become evident now.

*

The first day of November celebrates All Saints' Day, a Memorial Day in France. People go to the cemetery to pay a visit to their dead. They leave fresh flowers or pot plants on the tombstone. Some take time to scrub the family grave. At the graveyard doors, stalls sell white, purple or yellow chrysanthemums.

November is one of the gloomiest months of the year. Cold, rainy, sorrowful, it brings about the renewed sadness of losing the ones we loved.

Meeting Lisette on All Saints' Day, in Australia, on a mild spring morning, after twenty years away from one another was an uncanny combination of events. I was ill at ease. How would it feel to meet her again after so many years? Would I be disappointed by the way Janine Hosking portrayed my old friend? Would I see the same woman as the one I had known? I didn't feel like watching the documentary on my own. A close friend living nearby quickly understood my concerns. She offered a viewing at her place. My malaise slowly slipped away as I listened to Janine Hosking's interview of Philip Nitschke punctuated by her long dialogue with Lisette.

The first part of *Mademoiselle and the Doctor* follows Philip Nitschke's busy days as he drives across the wide, barren spaces of Australia, answers to a phone interview, listens to the anxious messages left on his answering machine and conducts the workshops of Exit International, the organisation he founded in 1997, with reassuring confidence. There, elderly men and women talk openly about the various methods they have heard of for ending their lives, asking Dr. Nitschke for advice. They are obviously relieved to be able to express their wish to die without reservation – a matter they cannot always disclose to their children, spouses, or GP. Some of them, terminally ill, speak with difficulty. Others are in relatively good health. All of them are adamant. Refusing to be kept alive against their will, they have come to the workshop for guidance, before they get trapped by illness or crippling dementia.

*

Lisette appears within a few minutes. My eyes are glued to the television screen. Lightly made-up, she is shot from a three-quarter view. As never before, I am struck by her dazzling personality. Dressed in a bright blue blouse to which is pinned a large gold brooch, she speaks with composure. Her perfect English rings with a strong French accent. Her abrasive humour makes me smile. Her thoughts sound right, grounded, authentic in an epoch when so many have lost the ability to say what they mean. She reminds me of a time when people spoke their mind. Not so long ago.

Seeing that she has to explain and somehow justify her decision in front of a camera, bearing in mind that her statement will be heard by anonymous citizens as well as leading statesmen and women, she handles the interview with startling self-control. A few minutes later, sitting in her study in front of her small typewriter, she drums the keys to compose her last statement with skilled swiftness, smacking each letter with the desperate energy of a writer racing against time. As she appears in the film, she is unmistakably the same person as the one I have known, talking about her decision with solemnity and humour, stating that death isn't depressing – it is a fact of life that should be accepted in good spirit.

*

In the footage, reminiscing about her childhood, she reverts to French. The melody of her voice, speaking our mother tongue, tips me over. The tension in my chest is suddenly creeping up my throat. Lisette is here, in front of me, more alive than ever.

Black and white images flick by. Lisette as a child standing beside her sister Lulu on the beach. Her grandmother, who raised the two girls, holding them in her arms.

Lisette isn't just speaking my mother tongue, she is talking about our beloved land. Unlike Lisette, I wasn't born close to the sea, but I've always lived near the ocean. As a child, my native town was less than an hour away from the beaches of the Atlantic coast and that's where I spent my summer holidays. I then settled in Perth, a city which opens onto the Indian Ocean, before moving to the Illawarra flanked by the Tasman Sea. But in my eyes, nothing compares to the Atlantic. It has no glamorous vistas, no stunning bright blue like that of the Indian Ocean, no exuberant vegetation like that of the Illawarra, no breath-taking lookouts. The Atlantic is a flat expanse of waters unfurling its subdued colours beneath a grey sky.

Here are unvarying landscapes of sweet-smelling maritime pines. Here are villages whose greyish stone houses huddle around a Romanesque church, beautiful in its simplicity. Here, a stone calvary erected at the crossing of two roads towers above salt marshes as green as rice fields. Here are poor lands swept by the wind, bringing in an intoxicating smell of iodine. Here, long sand beaches broaden at low tide their infinite stretches to invite the dreamer to walk. Here is the place to dream, think, a book in one's hand, carried away to other realms.

On our way to Lisbon, Thomas and I had made a trip to La Cotinière. We looked for Lisette's grandmother's house, or what was left of it. We walked the main street leading to the port. It was mid-August and the small island was packed with tourists. The bridge connecting Oléron to the mainland, built well after Lisette's time, had transformed this untamed windy place into a fashionable destination. As we were leaving, Thomas bought a postcard of La Cotinière and wrote his greetings before dropping the missive in a mail box. Although unstamped, the picture journeyed down to Australia and delighted Lisette; she told us so in her next letter. She couldn't locate her grandmother's house. She was nonetheless thrilled by the sight of the lighthouse, bright red, unchanged, the full-size toy of her childhood, blessed light guiding the fishing boats through the night.

I realise today how much the mystique of the native land, the *genius loci,* was sealed in Lisette's psyche. She had left Oléron at seventeen, travelled the world, lived and died in a faraway country, yet remained deeply connected to her small island. The ocean was her lifelong inspiration and a call for freedom from her earlier years spent in symbiosis with the land. I was born on the mainland – she was undoubtedly an islander. Strong-minded. Self-reliant. Fierce. Daring. Janine Hosking's documentary conveys a glimpse of this: Lisette appears standing at the far end of a wooden jetty, holding the railing, gazing at the sea, lost in contemplation. Her small silhouette shimmers between ocean and sky, an incandescent dot in the midst of silvery waters, a molten element amongst the elements.

*

After watching Janine Hosking's documentary, Lisette's visage imposes its vivid presence throughout the rest of that day. Her face is looming right above me. The following night, she comes back in my dream. She appears lying in a large coffin shining like black lacquer. Half of the side is clear and through this glass pane, I see the upper part of her body. There are only two people attending her funeral. Thomas and I.

Moving images have the power to snatch the dead out of their death. Time is compressed. Years collapse. On All Saints' Day, as I was watching the documentary shot in Trigg, I travelled back to the white bungalow. I re-entered Lisette's study, which opened onto a small terrace. I sat down beside her at the dining-table in the sunny corner, where she is shown near Dr Nitschke. I rediscovered the beige and brown armchairs. And slowly, progressively, something unseen and unheard emerged. I saw what I never saw before. I heard in Lisette's words what had I never paid attention to. She had a secret. Why didn't I realise it twenty years before?

The documentary was shot a few weeks before her death. How can she be so peaceful? How does she manage to be so serene and jovial? There is no self-pity, no whining, no doubt in her voice. No arrogance or boasting either. No narcissism. She beams with a youthful mirth and speaks with the lucidity of a sage. She answers the questions, however personal, without the slightest trace of irritation.

Will the scales fall from my eyes? Each day, I add another paragraph to my draft. Each day, I step a little closer, as though I were spinning around a nucleus. She holds my hand and draws me closer to where she stands, at the epicentre. Turning the conundrum around, I come up with a simpler answer, quite different from what I was seeking.

She was a woman in the presence of whom anyone felt comfortable. People were drawn to her sunny personality, because she didn't judge. She didn't pretend to be what she was not. She never bragged about her achievements, didn't blame others for her misfortune. She listened carefully to what I confided in her. And I can assert that Lisette was in real life as she appears in the film. Not a sweet little old lady: she shunned hypocrites and idle chatters, cherished her solitude. Humour was her wisdom, an offbeat sense of humour echoing her quirky nature. Humourists, I have heard, aren't always in their personal life what they portray on stage, as though humour were an elegant mask to cheat their sorrow.

Like a tree divested of its leaves, Lisette had been stripped of her joys and thrilling expectations. A disciple of Voltaire, I know that she was afflicted by the same 'joyful pessimism', veiling behind her mirth the secret wounds she never shared with me.

*

To my surprise, I discover that *Mademoiselle and the Doctor* had been shot partly before Lisette's death and partly after. Fifteen minutes before the end of the film, the atmosphere changes brutally. In the quiet of the night, a dog barks. The day is dawning in Trigg. The voice-over of a journalist reports that the retired university lecturer Lisette Nigot, a healthy and independent woman, had killed herself with lethal drugs she purchased overseas. In the following sequence, Philip Nitschke confronts the first online articles reporting Lisette's death, distressed to see that what was obviously a suicide has made the front page of the leading Australian newspapers. While watching Nitschke's tensed face, I cannot help remembering my own sadness and anger when I came across the same flood of articles in the small Internet café in Lisbon, and the consequent urge to write a letter to the editor of the *West Australian* stating that 'Our death belongs to us'. In actual fact, within a few days the country was swamped with articles, radio and television interviews portraying Lisette as the woman she wasn't. It looked very much like an orchestrated campaign to discredit Dr Nitschke. Lisette's name got tangled in the midst of it. John Howard, the prime minister at the time, expressed publicly his hostility towards advocates for rational suicide, adding his name to the long list of Philip Nitschke's detractors.

Even though Lisette had left the empty bottles of Seconal in full view, even though she had pinned a handwritten suicide note on the wall and typed a statement, a coronial inquest was conducted and the police opened an inquiry.

Why recall those ugly memories? Why recall our anger and our distress? Many years have gone by. Since 2002, the Parliament has legislated. The right to voluntary assisted dying has been voted on and has been passed in much of Australia, other than the Australian Capital Territory and the Northern Territory. We must acknowledge this advance, yet so many issues still need to be looked into. To be eligible for voluntary assisted dying, one needs to fit definite criteria. Many barriers and administrative formalities impede the process. People are asked to attend multiple in-person appointments with accredited doctors. The government has put a ban on using telemedicine which could ease and speed the procedure, overlooking the fact that most of those who apply for voluntary assisted dying are too sick to travel. Spending several hours in a car is an ordeal. People are still required to take a long drive with a family member or a friend, if there is someone available to take them, which makes it nearly impossible for those who live in the most isolated zones of Australia. This is followed by the emotional distress of weeks of waiting. The final deliverance they wish for seems to be granted as a privilege and not as a right, as Philip Nitschke explains. It is evident that there are still too many stumbling blocks for elderly and terminally ill people who apply for voluntary assisted dying, particularly if there is no one around to help them through the VAD request and administrative process.

Even though the law has changed, the law-makers are still unwilling to look into controversial issues, as though deaf to the questions raised by the *vox populi*.

People who are old, but not terminally ill, cannot have access to voluntary assisted dying. This was the case of Dr David Goodall. Sound of mind, having expressed his wish to die at the age of 104, Dr Goodall had nevertheless to fly from Australia to Switzerland in 2017 to be given a lethal injection.

One might wonder why many elderly people attend the workshops of Exit International? In our society, the majority of people die at the hospital. Dying at home, surrounded by loved ones, belongs to the past. Modern death is artificial. Modern death is cold and clinical. But how would we feel if we were caught against our will in a vortex of unnecessary and futile treatments to prolong our days, silenced by drugs and disempowered, if there is no friend or family to voice our concerns? For many of us, especially as we grow old, the perspective of being instrumentalised in the hands of a medical authority adds distress to our initial sense of hopelessness. Even though we might not be on our own at the time of death, we will face it alone. However strong we may be now, we don't know if we will be stoic or terrified when our hour comes, relieved to depart or unable to bear the idea of our own finitude. Alone, yes, and we might feel even lonelier as we lay on a sterile hospital bed rather than in our own bed at home.

This is why countless voices all over the world urge their governments to be granted the right to have control over their death.

*

Lisette had bared her soul at a vulnerable moment. It wasn't in vain. Her final statement was made not only to speak her truth but also with the strong hope 'that the circumstances may change to make it easier for others in the future'. A new law was bound to be adopted. And other laws will be voted. Lisette's voice was added to the hundreds of people who advocated for voluntary euthanasia, associations of all kind, families in distress. Thanks to them, some success has been achieved. Yet the campaigning continues. There is more work to be done.

Dr Philip Nitschke left Australia in 2016 after burning his medical practitioner's certificate, worn out by years of harassment. This put an end to his medical career. Yet Nitschke hasn't given up. He is still helping many elders to access a peaceful death. He was 'the first one in the world to administer a legal, voluntary lethal injection after which the patient activated the syringe using a computer'*. He was also the first in Australia to create an open space where people in physical or mental pain could talk without feeling guilt or shame about death and the will to die. Nitschke acknowledged their request, showing empathy and respecting their freedom. Freedom of speech. Freedom of choice. Freedom to die. My tribute to Lisette is also a tribute to the man she admired and regarded as a friend.

A large majority of people support voluntary euthanasia and rational suicide for elders all over the world. Yet many political leaders are deaf to their plight. Times have changed. Society has changed. As we have witnessed, however difficult it is to get hold of life-ending drugs, men and women who have decided to end their life will find

* Exit International website.

the means to do so whatever it costs to purchase the drugs or whatever it takes to fly to Switzerland.

And the day will come when the sovereignty of each person over their life and their death will be respected. One day will come when voluntary assisted dying and rational suicide, requiring a written statement drafted by the interested party, will be considered a basic human right. The Advance Care Directive* is a first step. Let's hope it will be a turning-point leading to new progressive laws.

*

As I drive home after watching the DVD, one brief sequence in the documentary keeps dogging me. At home, I replay the DVD. What troubles me is a note left by Lisette. No more than a few sentences. They are addressed to Philip Nitschke. The piece of paper screened in a shadowy frame is almost illegible in places. In the end, I have to take

* The Advance Care Directive is an official document that outlines personal values regarding end-of-life care and specifies treatments one does not wish to receive.

several pictures of the television screen to zoom in and figure out each word. The message reads as follow:

> *1a.m.*
> *Tell Philippe.*
> *Took me nearly 1H10*
> *to empty 200 capsules.*
> *The powder fills about 1/3 of a*
> *bowl and it takes about 1/2 litre of*
> *water to bring it to a drinkable stage.*
> *I hope I can make it.*
> *There must be an easier way!*

I can hardly recognise Lisette's handwriting. She would have been exhausted and in a state of emotional distress since the first name of Dr Nitschke is spelt as it is in French, Philippe.

Lisette's last words haunt me because what happened on the night of the 18th of November 2002 doesn't match the scenario I put together.

Indeed, I wasn't aware of the whole tragedy until I watched *Mademoiselle and the Doctor*. The reality often refutes what has been neatly meted out. The foot soldier who walks full of innocent enthusiasm to the battlefield isn't the man who lies bleeding in the trenches.

In the pages retracing Lisette's last week, her last day, I shamefully failed to perceive the agony of her last hours. I didn't specify the time spent in the kitchen to empty the 200 capsules, more than one hour, the anxiety drawing her to the brink of giving up, the feeling of hopelessness and the yearning to call for help, the terror of not being able to make it. Sitting on the edge of the bed, after she'd ingested half a litre of water thickened with barbiturates, queasy, holding down the nausea, she nevertheless braced herself to find enough courage, at 1 am, to write a note to Philip Nitschke, the only man to whom she could talk in earnest. *I hope I can make it. There must be an easier way!*

To Janine Hosking's question about terminating

one's life, Lisette answered that *it is not as easy as it sounds*. Before adding: *I wish it was behind me*. No, I didn't fully apprehend how much pain you would have to endure, Lisette. I hope you will forgive me. Yes, you were right, there should have been an easier way to die.

Suicide is usually regarded as a sign of utmost despair, an act carried out in a moment of folly. Had the person met the right friend on the fatal day, had they met the right doctor who would have prescribed the right treatment, the tragedy wouldn't have taken place. Suicide has been decriminalised only recently in Australia. Yet, a person attempting to end their life is still regarded by their fellow-citizens as *felo de se*, or 'a felon unto themself' as it used to be called by the law.

However, suicide isn't always related to folly or despair. Nor even to depression. We should remember that rational suicide wasn't born in our modern age. Called philosophical suicide in the ancient Greek world, it was vindicated when the person didn't want to endure the hardship of physical and mental pains related to old age. Elderly men and women were allowed to put an end to their *taedium vitae,* literally 'lassitude of life', without being shamed or criticised. Cato and Socrates chose to die by suicide. Their examplary death expresses the essence of Stoic philosophy expounded by Seneca. One could dispute that there aren't many people similar to Cato in our modern society. I would object that I have met many, unassuming elders bestowed with a stoic fortitude.

*

I am not an atheist. My faith is strong and sound. Yet today, if I were asked about the meaning of life and death, I wouldn't be able to provide a valid answer because I am human, prone to making mistakes and fraught with doubts.

For many years, Lisette's decision to terminate her life had remained an unknown. I entirely respected her choice, but rational suicide still upset my principles. My unyielding past convictions have lost their harsh contours. Experience, pain and understanding have come to shift them.

If I were compelled to endure a life I would end up loathing, experiencing the lassitude of life, I would hesitate at the crossroad of my destiny, asking as Lisette did, 'What's the point of living when there is nothing to live for?' And there, pondering, I am unsure whether I would be prepared to pursue my journey according to God's will, or if I would choose to sever the thread of my days. I know that I would consider either road, regarding both as equally arduous.

The path of rational suicide isn't less righteous than the path of enduring. The path of enduring isn't more virtuous than the path of rational suicide.

I believe that no authority whatsoever, neither religious, nor political, nor medical, has the right to coerce anyone to stay on this planet against their will, and by adding physical pain to their existential pain, transform their life into a long-lasting torture as they wait for their life to end. Those who judge and reprove anyone who takes their life might not have reached yet a 'sad old age', as Ovid called it. They may not know whether one day, if excruciating pain torments their body or if a state of profound existential despair shatters theirs hopes, they will not beseech a charitable hand, human or divine, to put an end to their suffering, unable to go on any further.

*

At the tail end of Janine Hosking's film, somewhere in the Northern Territory, sitting in a folding chair, his eyes shaded by protective glasses, Philip Nitschke contemplates the sky. Beside the glowing embers of a fire, he patiently waits to marvel at a solar eclipse. He has driven great distances to watch it, he explains. Nitschke is a man of few words. He looks up, holding a pair of binoculars. The sun is disappearing. Night is slowly falling over the desert. Nitschke, breathless, cannot hold back a smile. It is needless to write long treatises. Pointing at the mind-blowing fading of the sun behind the perfect eye of the moon is more explicit than any lengthy talk. It shows us how insignificant we are, Dr Nitschke comments. No one has yet figured out the miracle of life. But the enigma of death hasn't been cracked either. Philip Nitschke didn't need words to understand you, Lisette. You shared the same secret. You too trusted in the benevolence of the universe. You too believed in the great spirit of the world.

*

Sweet Lisette, I've lingered many years before I could carry out my task, to close your coffin of wind and sand. You came back one morning waving your canvas hat from the deck of the boat, having left me on the shore. You have been at once a strong and a gentle warrior. You have been the drop flowing down the river, the river returning to the ocean. The sea never judged you and Mother Death has not either. You have walked towards her as you would have walked to a fête where you'd be queen. Your ashes were scattered in the cove you cherished. You've gently disembarked on a faraway beach, on a small island anchored in the Atlantic. You've alighted in the peaceful and burning time of life when we finally let go of everything with no more war to wage, and no more hate to feed. A time of absolute certainty. An encompassing love has carried away the tiny piece of flesh you have been, in all its goodness, in all your goodness. You have entered an everlasting day wrapped in an unbounded whole.

In the warm afternoon when we sit side by side in the low brown armchairs, holding your discoloured Polaroids in your tiny hand, you whisper, 'I am glad to have met you, kid. I loved our conversations. We didn't have enough time though. One more thing before I go. Do not cling to what is around you, for what is around will pass and disappear. Do not cling to people. They too will pass and disappear. At the time of death, you'll think: so much effort to end up empty-handed. If you still cling desperately to your existence, remember that life is an inn we pass briefly through, hosted for the night, gone the next morning. We fail to recall that we are trivial dust and frail wanderers. We are a puff of wind and grain of sand. Our life flies by in a blink. Within a few weeks, we are forgotten. Remember that everything will be swept away. The names will fade. The faces will recede in the distance. The names of the politicians who drafted merciless laws will be forgotten. Other politicians will come after them. They will draft new laws, and they'll be forgotten in turn. Other generations will be born, will grow old, and will die and the names and faces will be forgotten. One day, you will understand. You will understand that I am at peace. I look straight at the sun. Because where I am, there is no solitude. Where I am, kid, there is no pain.'

Lisette Nigot's Final Statement

'I am neither terminally ill nor in pain or depressed and I am sound of mind. However, I am terminating my life by way of voluntary euthanasia by taking a drug which I hope will ensure a gentle, rapid, painless death. I procured this drug from abroad knowing that the oppressive laws of this country do not allow for freedom of choice in matters of life and death. Why is there such pressure against helping or allowing people who have had enough of living, who often suffer extreme pain and wish to put an end to it to fulfil their longing for final peace? I am terminating my life now because I want to have control over my death. If voluntary euthanasia were legal, if it were possible to make arrangements to obtain the necessary assistance and control when it becomes obvious that one's condition has reached the point where there is no longer quality of life, then I might wait for that moment to request to be helped to die in a human way but since lawful assistance to die is not accepted in this cowardly restricted society, I am taking the matter into my own hands hoping that the circumstances may change to make it easier for others in the future.'

Mademoiselle Lisette Nigot left a Memorial Prize to the University of Western Australia where she lectured for twenty years. The annual income of $8000 is donated to the university to support outstanding students of the French language.

*

Janine Hosking received the Australian International Documentary Conference's Stanley Hawes Award in 2020, for her Outstanding Contribution to the documentary sector in Australia. The DVD of her documentary *Mademoiselle and the Doctor* is available on the Exit International website.

*

‘On 27 November 2015, Dr Nitschke formally burned his medical registration certificate in Darwin, ending a twenty-five-year career in medicine. Philip left Australia for a new life in Europe in January 2016.’ (Philip Nitschke’s website)

ACKNOWLEDGEMENTS

My gratitude goes to my publisher Xavier Hennekinne, who, over the years has never stopped believing in my work. His sincere support and trust gave me strength. Many thanks to Lenka Miklos who helped me deepen each thought while I was writing this book. Working with Xavier and Lenka has been a joy.

I thank Hugh Riminton for his precious suggestions.

Many thanks to Laure Liss, Elizabeth Inglis, and the members of the Dying with Dignity association, for their invaluable advice throughout the writing of this book.

I wish to express my gratitude and admiration to Dr Philip Nitschke. His example, his courage and his spirit helped me complete this text in homage to our friend, Lisette.